Native Americans

The Miwok

Barbara A. Gray-Kanatiiosh

ABDO Publishing Company

visit us at
www.abdopublishing.com

Published by ABDO Publishing Company, 8000 West 78th Street, Edina, Minnesota 55439. Copyright © 2002 by Abdo Consulting Group, Inc. International copyrights reserved in all countries. No part of this book may be reproduced in any form without written permission from the publisher.

Printed in the United States of America, North Mankato, Minnesota.
012002 052012

Illustrations: David Kanietakeron Fadden
Interior Photos: Corbis
Editors: Bob Italia, Tamara L. Britton, Kate A. Conley, Kristin Van Cleaf
Art Direction & Maps: Neil Klinepier

Library of Congress Cataloging-in-Publication Data

Gray-Kanatiiosh, Barbara A., 1963-
   The Miwok / Barbara A. Gray-Kanatiiosh
     p. cm. -- (Native Americans)
Includes index.
   Summary: An introduction to the history, social life and customs, and present life of the Miwok Indians, a tribe in California.
    ISBN 1-57765-601-6
   1. Miwok Indians--History--Juvenile literature. 2. Miwok Indians--Social life and customs--Juvenile literature. [1. Miwok Indians. 2. Indians of North America--California.] I. Title. II. Native Americans (Edina, Minn.)

E99.M69 G73 2002
979. 4'0049741--dc21
                                                      2001045894

About the Author: Barbara A. Gray-Kanatiiosh, JD

Barbara Gray-Kanatiiosh, JD, is an Akwesasne Mohawk. She has a Juris Doctorate from Arizona State University, where she was one of the first recipients of ASU's special certificate in Indian Law. She is currently pursuing a Ph.D. in Justice Studies at ASU and is focusing on Native American issues. Barbara works hard to educate children about Native Americans through her writing and Web site where children may ask questions and receive a written response about the Haudenosaunee culture. The Web site is: www.peace4turtleisland.org

Illustrator: David Kanietakeron Fadden

David Kanietakeron Fadden is a member of the Akwesasne Mohawk Wolf Clan. His work has appeared in publications such as *Akwesasne Notes, Indian Time*, and the *Northeast Indian Quarterly*. Examples of his work have appeared in various publications of the Six Nations Indian Museum in Onchiota, NY. His work has also appeared in "How The West Was Lost: Always The Enemy," produced by Gannett Production which appeared on the Discovery Channel. David's work has been exhibited in Albany, NY; the Lake Placid Center for the Arts; Centre Strathearn in Montreal, Quebec; North Country Community College in Saranac Lake, NY; Paul Smith's College in Paul Smiths, NY; and at the Unison Arts & Learning Center in New Paltz, NY.

Contents

Where They Lived 4

Society 6

Food 8

Homes 10

Clothing 12

Crafts 14

Family 16

Children 18

Myths 20

War 22

Contact with Europeans 24

Chief Tenaya 26

The Miwok Today 28

Glossary 30

Web Sites 31

Index 32

Where They Lived

The traditional Miwok (MEE-wuk or MEE-wahk) homeland was in central California. Their land base was very large. It was home to different groups of Miwok.

The Coast Miwok lived north of present-day San Francisco and San Pablo Bay. The Lake Miwok lived on the land stretching from southeast of Clear Lake all the way to present-day Pope Valley. The Eastern Miwok lived on the land that included the Sierra Nevada mountains, Mount Diablo, and the present-day cities of Sacramento and Compton.

Miwok homelands had many types of land. Grasslands, valleys, and oak forests made up the land. There were also lakes, marshes, streams, and rivers. The Pacific Ocean, beaches, and bays bordered the Coast Miwok's homelands.

The Miwoks spoke Miwokan languages. Miwokan languages come from the Utian language family, of the Penutian language group.

The hills around Mount Diablo

The Miwok Homelands

DETAIL AREA

North
West — East
South

5

Society

    The Miwok lived in settlements called tribelets. A tribelet was an independent group with its own territory. Each tribelet was made up of several permanent settlements. The settlements each had leaders, advisers, and healers who did different jobs.

    Some Miwok settlements had **hereditary** leaders. Other settlements chose their leaders. Male leaders were called *hoypuh* (HOY-poo). Female leaders were called *hoypuh kuleyih* (HOY-poo COOL-ey-ye). The leaders advised and protected the people. They also organized hunting, fishing, and trading events.

    A *maien* (MEY-en) was a female spiritual leader. She was in charge of the ceremonial house. She prepared food and organized ceremonies. *Maiens* picked dancers and singers and sent out invitations for people to attend the ceremonies.

    Medicine people healed and conducted group ceremonies. There were different kinds of medicine people. Deer doctors could **foretell** good hunts. Singing doctors used songs to heal.

Sucking doctors received messages in their dreams telling them how to heal patients. It is said they could suck out the illness. Other medicine people used plants to heal.

A Miwok tribelet settlement

Food

The Miwok hunted, fished, and gathered their foods. For tribelets along the coast, the ocean provided **kelp** and seafood such as clams and mussels. The Miwok used shell and bone hooks, and woven traps and nets to catch fish such as sturgeon and salmon.

Inland, the Miwok hunted with bows and arrows, traps, nets, slingshots, and bolas. They hunted deer, elk, rabbits, and birds such as quail and geese. Then the women prepared the meat. They roasted it, dried it, or cooked it on a stick over a fire. They stored the dried meat and fish to eat during the winter.

The Miwok also gathered acorns. Acorns were a major part of the Miwok diet. Miwok stored their harvested acorns in granaries. They pounded the acorns into **meal**, which could be made into mush or bread.

The Miwok gathered seeds as well. They collected them by hitting plants with seed beaters. This knocked the seeds into collecting baskets. Then the Miwok roasted the seeds.

In addition to gathering acorns and seeds, the Miwok gathered berries, greens, clover, and bulbs. To do this, they used digging sticks with fire-hardened tips. The Miwok also ate roasted grasshoppers and yellow jacket **grubs**.

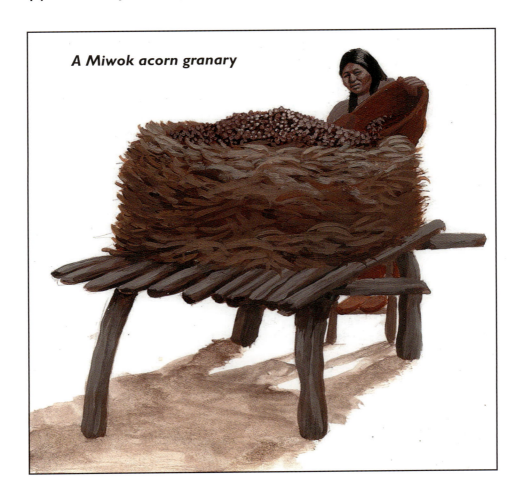

A Miwok acorn granary

Homes

The various Miwok tribes lived in different types of homes. The Lake Miwok lived in round, multi-family homes. They built these houses over a pit and used poles as the framework. They covered the frames with brush, leaves, and **tule** (TOO-lee).

The Eastern Miwok lived in cone-shaped homes made of long strips of bark. Other Eastern Miwok families made similar homes by arranging poles in cone shapes. They covered the poles with brush, grass, and tule.

The Coast Miwok lived in cone-shaped houses, too. First, they made a frame from willow or driftwood poles. Then they leaned additional poles against the frame for strength. Last, they covered the sides with grass, **rushes**, or tule.

Some Miwok also built large roundhouses. To make a roundhouse, the Miwok first dug a pit. This pit formed the walls. Then the Miwok buried logs in the ground around the pit to form a frame. The frame supported a roof made of smaller poles and earth.

All Miwok homes had a central fire pit. They used the pit to heat the home and cook meals. Miwok made their beds from **tule** and their pillows from grass. They used furs and skins for blankets. Some Miwok also lined the floors with pine needles or bay leaves.

An Eastern Miwok home

A Lake Miwok home

A Coast Miwok home

Clothing

    In the summer, the Miwok wore very little clothing. Men occasionally wore **breechcloths** made from deer **hide**. Sometimes they wore sleeveless **tule** shirts or deer hides thrown over their shoulders.

    Women wore skirts made from shredded tule, grass, or deer hide. Some Miwok women wore dresses made from single pieces of deer hide. Women and men both went barefoot.

    In the colder months, the Miwok wore fur robes. They also wore woven, rabbit fur blankets.

    Miwok men and women **tattooed** their chins. They used ashes and a sharp piece of flint or **obsidian** to make these tattoos. The tattoos were usually lines drawn downward from the mouth. Some Miwok tattoos began at the chin and went down to the chest.

A Miwok family wearing traditional clothing

Both men and women usually wore their hair long. They brushed their hair with brushes made of soaproot fibers. For special occasions, men wore hair nets. The Miwok also wore necklaces and ear jewelry made from bones or shells.

Crafts

    The Miwok were skilled craftspeople. They used items from their environment to make things they needed. For example, they made shell beads to use as money and jewelry.

    To make money beads, Miwok craftspeople first broke clam shells into cubes. Then they drilled a hole in the center of each cube. Finally, they shaped and polished the cubes by rubbing them on rocks.

    To make bead jewelry, the Miwok used haliotis, olivella, and abalone shells. They made the shells into beads and **pendants**.

    The Miwok were also skilled basketmakers. They made **twined** seed beater baskets from willow. Seed beaters had long handles and spoon-shaped ends.

    Basketmakers made coiled baskets from willow, sedge root, and redbud bark. The Miwok used these baskets for gathering, cooking, and storage. They decorated these coil baskets with feathers, shell beads, and abalone **pendants**. The Miwok also used these baskets for ceremonies and gifts.

Men made bows and arrows. They made the bows from hazel, oak, or dogwood. They made the bow strings from **sinew** or **hemp**. They made arrows from ash, oak, or willow branches. They rubbed the branches on a grooved stone to make them straight. They attached the arrowheads with sinew or leather.

A Miwok woman uses a seed beater basket to harvest seeds.

Family

    Miwok marriages were often arranged. To arrange a marriage, a man's family gave gifts to a woman's family. If the woman's family accepted the gifts, they gave gifts to the man's family. This showed they approved of the marriage.

    Miwok families usually included a mother, a father, and children. Grandparents, aunts, uncles, and cousins often lived in the same home or nearby in the village. Men and women had specific jobs to ensure their families' survival.

    The men hunted and fished. On a deer hunt, the men disguised themselves with deer heads and **hide** capes. They walked slowly up to the deer herd. When a hunter came close enough to a deer, he shot it with an arrow.

    To catch smaller game, such as rabbits, the men made brush fences. They set up a handwoven net inside each fence. The villagers chased the animals into the net. Then they killed the rabbits with clubs. After a successful hunt, the men took the animals back to the village.

When the men returned, the women butchered the animals the men had killed. They also used the **hides** and furs to make clothing.

It was also the women's job to gather the Miwok's food, such as acorns. The women gathered acorns from the ground or knocked them from the trees with sticks. They shelled the nuts and spread their meats on the ground to dry.

When the acorns were dry, the women pounded them into flour. Then they washed the flour to remove the bitter taste. When the bitterness was gone, they used the acorn **meal** to make soup, mush, and bread.

Miwok hunters use a brush net to capture game.

Children

    The Miwok carried their babies in cradle baskets. They wove willow or **tule** to form U-shaped carriers. A strap allowed the mother to carry her baby in the basket on her back.

    Children began working with their elders at a young age. This way, they learned the skills needed to ensure their families' survival. Young boys learned how to make and use bows and arrows, nets, and **snares**. They also learned to make **rabbit sticks**.

    Young girls learned how to find and gather the materials needed to make baskets. They also learned how to prepare acorns and make acorn soup, mush, and bread. Both boys and girls helped the women gather greens, fruits, and berries.

    Tribelet elders and family taught boys and girls about the Miwok traditions. They learned the songs, dances, and stories of their **culture**.

Miwok children also had time to play. They played, ran, and swam. They played with tops made from acorns. Girls played with mud or stick dolls with **tule** skirts.

Children played a type of handball. To play the game, the children used a ball of angelica leaves. The players stood in a circle. They used their hands to hit the ball to another player. If the player missed the ball, he or she was out. The last person left was the winner.

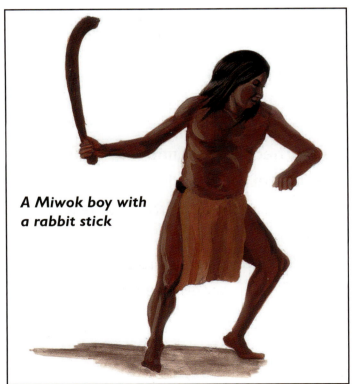

A Miwok boy with a rabbit stick

Myths

The following is a Miwok creation story. It tells how Old Man Coyote created the land and people.

Old Man Coyote told Frog that he wanted to create people. Frog was pleased, but he said, "Water is not a good place for people to live." Old Man Coyote nodded his head in agreement. Old Man Coyote said to Frog, "Frog, please swim down to the ocean floor and bring me some mud."

Frog dove into the water. After awhile he came up breathless. Frog said, "Old Man Coyote, I can't reach the bottom." Old Man Coyote said, "Try again, please."

Frog dived three more times, but failed to bring up any mud. After the third time he lay floating on the water, resting. As Frog lay there, Old Man Coyote looked down at Frog's legs and saw a speck of mud.

Old Man Coyote picked up the mud. He took out a **tule** blanket and shook the soil to the north, south, east, and west. As he shook his blanket, the mud grew and became land.

Now that there was land, Old Man Coyote could make people. He picked up sticks and placed them in the earth. Each stick was set in a different area and given a name. Old Man Coyote waved his blanket over the sticks and they became people. This is how Old Man Coyote created the land and people.

Old Man Coyote

War

Keeping peace with other tribes was very important to the Miwok's survival. They traded with other tribes for things they needed. The Miwok could not trade with tribes they were at war with. So they tried to keep the peace.

Because they needed to keep peace with other tribes, war was rare. When war did occur, the Miwok used many of the same tools they used for hunting and fishing as weapons.

Some Miwok used long, mahogany-handled spears as weapons. Each spear handle had an **obsidian** spearhead attached to one end. Obsidian is sometimes called volcanic glass, and is very sharp.

Other Miwok warriors used bows and arrows as weapons. Some Miwok made two-part arrows. The front of the arrow had a hardwood shaft. The back part was made of reed. When an enemy was shot and tried to pull out the arrow, it came apart, leaving the arrowhead inside the body.

The Miwok also used bolas and slingshots. Each bola was five to seven long pieces of rope. A bone was tied to the end of each rope. When the warrior threw the bola, it wrapped itself around the target. Bolas were mostly used for hunting birds and small animals, but could also be used to confuse enemies. Slingshots fired hard, sundried clay pellets.

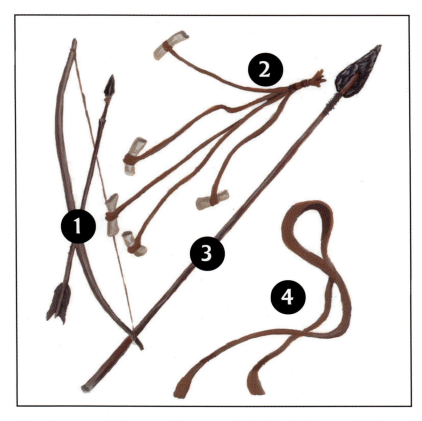

Miwok weapons: 1. Bow and arrow 2. Bola 3. Spear 4. Slingshot

Contact with Europeans

In the 1500s, Queen Elizabeth I of England sent Sir Francis Drake on an **expedition** against the Spanish colonies. In 1579, Drake brought his ship, the *Golden Hind*, into a bay north of present-day San Francisco for repairs. When Drake arrived, he met the Coast Miwok.

The Coast Miwok believed Drake and his men to be their dead ancestors. So they welcomed Drake and his men. Drake claimed the Coast Miwok lands for England and called it Nova Albion.

In the late 1700s, Spaniards began to settle in Miwok territory. The Spaniards built **missions**. They captured many Miwok and brought them to these missions. The Miwok were forced to work on the missions. The Spaniards forced the Miwok to give up their traditional beliefs and become Christians.

The Miwok faced problems for many years after the arrival of the Europeans. In the 1840s, settlers, traders, and gold miners brought illnesses the Miwok had no natural defenses against. Many Miwok died.

In 1850, California became part of the United States. The Miwok lost much of their land to American settlers. The U.S. military searched for Miwok people to drive them from the land they once lived on.

A Coast Miwok welcomes Sir Francis Drake

Chief Tenaya

Chief Tenaya (TEE-nah-yah) was a Yosemite Miwok. He was born in about 1830. When he was a young man, a grizzly bear attacked him. Tenaya fought for his life. He used a tree limb to kill the bear.

The Yosemite Miwok lands contained a large amount of gold. Miners and settlers came to Miwok lands to mine the gold. Fights over land soon began between the Miwok and the miners and settlers.

In the 1850s, the U.S. government tried to force the Miwok to give up their lands. U.S. troops destroyed acorn granaries and other food stored by the Miwok. The Miwok resisted, but eventually they were forced to move to the Fresno River **Reservation**.

In 1851, Tenaya led his people in an escape. He wanted to live free and return to Yosemite Valley, where the ashes of his ancestors were spread. U.S. troops tried to capture Tenaya and his people.

Many neighboring tribes joined Tenaya to fight against the gold miners and U. S. troops. Many Native Americans were killed in the fighting. So Tenaya called a **truce** and signed a peace treaty.

It is said that in 1853, under truce, Tenaya's people were **ambushed**. Tenaya died in the ambush. But many of his people escaped and fled into the Sierra Nevada mountains.

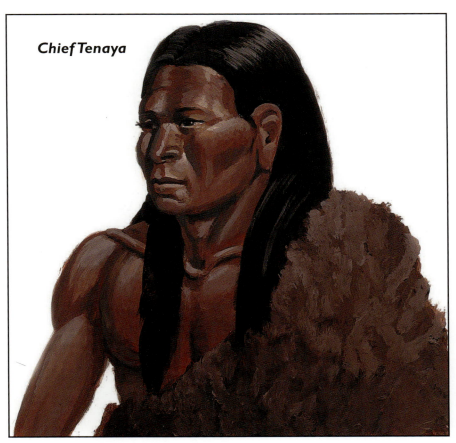

Chief Tenaya

The Miwok Today

Today, there are about 3,500 Miwok. California's Buena Vista, Chicken Ranch, Jackson **Rancherias** of Mi-Wuk Indians, Shingle Springs Band of Miwok Indians, and Graton Rancheria, are federally recognized groups.

Many Miwok live on rancherias. But other Miwok groups do not have any land. They are fighting legal battles to regain their lands and be officially recognized as tribes.

The Miwok are working to restore their languages and strengthen their traditional **cultural** ways. Today, many Miwok get together to dance and sing at the Big Time Festival held each July.

Today, there are Miwok living on rancherias in California. They also live in other parts of the world. Many have become teachers, lawyers, or doctors. Many Miwok children are learning their tribe's stories, dances, and songs so their culture will continue.

The California coastline just north of San Francisco in Coast Miwok traditional homelands

The Sacramento Valley, near Sacramento, in Eastern Miwok traditional homelands

29

Glossary

ambush - a surprise attack from a hidden position.

breechcloth - a piece of cloth wrapped between the legs and tied with a belt around the waist.

culture - the customs, arts, and tools of a nation or people at a certain time.

expedition - a journey taken for a special purpose.

foretell - to tell or know something before it happens.

grub - a young insect, usually a beetle, that resembles a worm.

hemp - a strong, tough fiber obtained from the stem of the hemp plant.

hereditary - passed on to later generations in a family.

hide - an animal skin that is often thick and heavy.

kelp - a brown seaweed that grows along the coasts of the Atlantic and Pacific Oceans.

meal - coarsely ground seeds.

mission - a center or headquarters for religious work.

obsidian - a hard, glassy rock formed when molten lava cools.

pendant - a hanging ornament.

rabbit stick - a weapon thrown at a running rabbit's legs that snares the legs and trips the rabbit, keeping it from running away so the hunter can catch it.

rancheria - a Native American village.

reservation - a piece of land set aside by the government for Native Americans to live on.

rush - a reedlike plant with a slender, hollow stem that grows in marshy areas.

sinew - a band of tough fibers that joins a muscle to a bone.

snare - a trap used to capture animals that is often a loop of rope hung from a tree.

tatoo - to permanently mark the skin with figures or designs.

truce - an agreement by opposing forces to stop fighting.

tule - a type of reed that grows in wetlands. Tule is native to California.

twine - to form by twisting, interweaving, or interlacing.

Web Sites

Graton Rancheria
http://www.coastmiwok.com
Visit the Graton Rancheria of Coast Miwok at this site. Learn about Coast Miwok history and culture. This site has many links to other Native American sites.

Miwok Archaeological Preserve of Marin
http://www.mapom.com
A great site with information about the Coast Miwok.

These sites are subject to change. Go to your favorite search engine and type in Miwok for more sites.

Index

B
beds 11
blankets 11, 12

C
ceremonies 6, 15
children 16, 18, 19
clothing 12, 17
cooking 8, 9, 11, 14, 17, 18
cradle baskets 18
crafts 14, 15

D
dances 6, 18, 28
Drake, Sir Francis 24

E
elders 18
Elizabeth I (Queen of England) 24
English 24

F
family 10, 16, 17, 18
festivals 28
fishing 6, 8, 16
food 6, 8, 9, 11, 16, 17, 18

G
games 19
gathering 8, 9, 14, 17, 18
gifts 15, 16

H
hair 13
homelands 4, 24, 25, 26, 28
homes 10, 11
hunting 6, 8, 16, 22, 23

I
illness 25

J
jewelry 13, 14

L
language 4, 28
leaders 6, 26, 27

M
marriage 16
medicine people 6, 7
missions 24
money 14

P
pillows 11

R
rancherias 28
reservations 26
roundhouses 10

S
settlers 24, 25, 26, 27
songs 18, 28
Spanish 24
storage 8, 14
stories 18, 20, 21, 28

T
tattoos 12
Tenaya (Chief) 26, 27
trading 6, 22
traps 8
tribelet 6, 8, 18

U
U. S. government 26
U.S. military 25, 26, 27

W
war 22, 23
weapons 8, 15, 18, 22, 23